CONTENTS

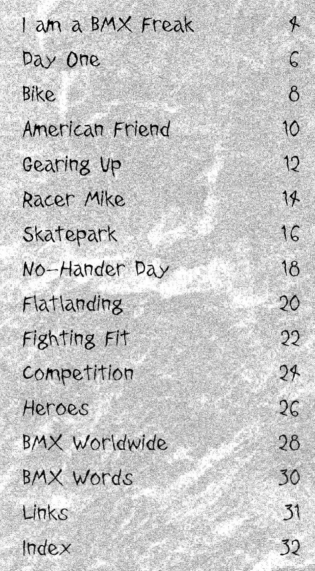

BMX words are explained on page 30.

I AM A BMX FREAK

Tyler Andrews Fact File
Age: Sixteen
Occupation: School student and BMX freak
Likes: Britney, Philip Pullman
Dislikes: Christina, J K Rowling
Music: Metal
Hobbies: BMX, free-running, flower arranging*
*delete one of the above

This is me.

This is the story of how I rose through the ranks. Once I was a dork: I didn't even know what a Superman was, let alone how to do one. I played sports with the other kids, did my schoolwork, ate my dinner and generally lived an ordinary life.

Me later in my BMX career.

Then I discovered BMX: the joy of riding a bike with a small frame and 20-inch wheels. One go on a friend's bike, and I was hooked. I was still a kook, of course, but now I was a kook with something to aim at. I wanted to be a decent freestyle BMX rider. This book, made up of bits and pieces typed, scribbled, stuck and pinned into my diary, tells the story of how I became a BMX freak.

Diary

of a

BMX

Freak

Heinemann
LIBRARY

www.heinemann.co.uk/
Visit our website to find out m
Library books.

To order:
☎ Phone 44 (0) 1865 888066
▤ Send a fax to 44 (0) 1865 3140
▭ Visit the Heinemann Bookshop) browse our
catalogue and order online.

Produced by Monkey Puzzle Media Ltd
Gissing's Farm, Fressingfield, Suffolk IP21 5SH, UK

First published in Great Britain by Heinemann
Library, Halley Court, Jordan Hill, Oxford
OX2 8EJ, part of Harcourt Education.
Heinemann is a registered trademark of Harcourt
Education Ltd.

This paperback edition published in 2005
© Monkey Puzzle Media Ltd 2004
The moral right of the proprietor has been asserted.

Author: Paul Mason
Editorial: Otto De'ath
Series Designer: Mayer Media Ltd
Book Designer: Mayer Media Ltd
Illustrator: Sam Lloyd
Production: Séverine Ribierre

Originated by Repro Multi-Warna
Printed in China by WKT Company Limited

ISBN 0 431 17542 X (hardback)
08 07 06 05 04
10 9 8 7 6 5 4 3 2 1

ISBN 0 431 17547 0 (paperback)
09 08 07 06 05
10 9 8 7 6 5 4 3 2 1

**British Library Cataloguing in Publication
Data**
Mason, Paul
Diary of a BMX Freak
796.6'3
A full catalogue record for this book is available
from the British Library.

Acknowledgements
With thanks to **Buzz Pictures** for supplying all
photographs.

Attention!

This book is about BMX, which is a dangerous sport. This book is
not a substitute for proper lessons. Readers are advised to get
lessons from a qualified instructor, always wear the right safety
equipment, and never ride alone.

Mat Hoffman
in action.

RIDING HERO - MAT HOFFMAN

The greatest BMX ramp rider ever, no question, with a major influence on shaping the sport:

• Contest winner and organizer, Mat is the inventor of some of the most radical tricks ever on a bike.

• Mat has starred in countless videos, adverts and magazines. He also owns and runs a successful BMX company, Hoffman Bikes.

• Mat also helped develop the famous game 'Mat Hoffman's Pro BMX'.

MARCH

1	8	15	22	29
2	9	16	23	30
3	10	17	24	31
4	11	18	25	
5	12	19	26	
6	13	20	(27)	
7	14	21	28	

DAY ONE

My mate Dave finally got me to go with him to a local BMX spot. He's been trying to persuade me for weeks, after I said BMX wasn't that hard and anyone who could ride a bike could learn it really easily. Boy, was I wrong!

Dave lent me his old bike, which is a bit banged up and kept clicking every time I stood on the pedals. He says it's the bottom bracket. Anyway, we got to the place and suddenly Dave started doing all this mad stuff, jumping up on to things, bouncing around on his back wheel, and leaping over obstacles. I couldn't do any of it at first, but finally he stopped jumping about and taught me how to do a bunny hop.

My first bunny hop (on camera, anyway!). You push on the pedal to get the front wheel up, then push the handlebars forwards to bring the rest of the bike up behind it.

6

Just as I was feeling pleased with myself, Dave pulled off this wall ride...

Fantasic Superman aerial!

SECRET LANGUAGE OF BMX:

BMX Stands for Bicycle Motocross.

Cross-up Turning the bars 180° in either direction.

Fakie Landing backwards.

Peg grind A trick where the bike's pegs grind along the edge of an obstacle.

Stoked Very pleased or excited by something.

JUNE

	7	14	21	28
1	8	15	22	29
2	9	16	23	30
3	10	17	24	
4	11	18	25	
5	12	19	(26)	
6	13	20	27	

Proud owner of new bike!

Always keep your helmet clean.

BIKE

After months of riding Dave's old bike (thank you, Dave!), it hardly seems possible I have my own. But I have. It's a shiny red number, set up just how I wanted. We ended up getting it as a build-up on a frame that I really liked.

The guys at the local BMX store were so helpful — they ride BMX themselves, so they were really keen to make sure I was happy with my new bike. Because I bought the whole bike from them it was far cheaper than if I'd bought the bits one at a time. There are still some bits and pieces I need to get, though: pegs, mainly, for when I want to do grinds. But also some other trick bits I've got my eye on!

BASIC SAFETY GEAR:

• Helmet — because a broken head might not mend!

• Gloves — for those nasty 'hands-out' scrapes.

• Long-sleeved top and jeans — give arms and legs protection from scrapes.

• Neoprene shin and knee pads can be worn under jeans.

• Hard-capped pads add more protection for ramp work.

8

HANDLEBARS WITH A 6-7"
RISE GIVE GOOD CONTROL.

SEAT SET LOW TO AVOID
IT GETTING IN THE WAY
WHILE DOING TRICKS.

20" WHEELS HAVE LESS
WEIGHT AND ACCELERATE
FASTER THAN STANDARD,
LARGER BIKE WHEELS.

HEAVY SPOKE
LACING ADDS
STRENGTH.

SINGLE-SPEED
GEARING IS SIMPLER,
AND ALLOWS THE
RIDER TO CONTROL
THE BIKE MORE
EFFECTIVELY.

COMPACT FRAME IS
STRONGER AND MORE
MANOEUVERABLE.

STRAIGHT FORKS FOR
MORE STRENGTH AND
RESPONSIVE STEERING.

5	12	19	26
6	13	20	27
7	14	21	28
1	8	15	22	29
2	9	16	23	30
3	10	17	24	31
4	11	18	25	

AMERICAN FRIEND

Inbox | Compose | Addresses | Folders | Options

Reply | Reply All | Forward | Delete | Previous | Next | Close

From: Zack Walters
To: Tyler Andrews
Subject: Greetings from USA
Date: Friday, July 9

Hey Tyler, good to get your email. Yep, I'm a BMX freak too, though it sounds like I've been doing it a while longer than you. I've attached a set of photos of me at one of our local spots. This is a place we ride quite a lot, though my younger brother Mike doesn't come as often now. He's gotten really into BMX racing, which is a big scene here in the US. Personally I can't stand it – give me a big skatepark any day, rather than riding round and round in circles. But I guess Mike might tell you different.

Anyhow, let me know how you're getting on. If you can get hold of a digital camera, send some photos.

Zack.

PS I sent you a little file about The Gonz – check out what he's saying about 'why do we call it BMX?'

PPS Your sister says hi!

Zack at his local BMX spot.

DAVE'S FEEBLE GRIND:

1 Bunny hop up to the height of the grind.

2 Land with the front wheel and the rear peg on the obstacle.

3 Let your momentum carry you forwards.

4 You could just return to Earth still going forwards. Dave performs a tailwhip to land fakie, before spinning round again to roll off forwards.

Zack's photos didn't come out but we shot this sequence of Dave doing a feeble grind.

'The Gonz' in action.

	Download Manager		
	Complete	< 1 minute	1.3 MB

Name: Mark Gonzales (a.k.a. 'The Gonz')
Type of riding: street
Based: Arizona, USA
Riding since: three years old
Influences: skateboarding
Quote: 'I really don't like the term "BMX". BMX stands for "bicycle motocross". What does that have to do with some kid hopping curbs on his way to the store? Nothing.'

11

AUGUST

2	9	16	23	30
3	10	17	24	31
4	11	18	25	
5	12	19	26	
6	13	20	27	
7	14	21	28	
1 8	15	22	29	

GEARING UP

Just back from practising with Dave and our friend Pete. We're all trying to get a couple of tricks totally wired before our trip to a really big skatepark nearby, at the weekend. Pete's still way better than me, but I think I'm catching him up a little bit.

I feel much more comfortable on the bike now – not tense every time I go for a trick. Pete reckoned it's because I've fallen off a few times. You pick up scrapes and the odd bruise, but you soon learn that falling off doesn't necessarily hurt that much. Especially if you're wearing pads! Of course, people do hurt themselves – one boy last weekend managed to break his arm trying a big jump...

FUFANU
THIS FELT LIKE A MASSIVE TRICK THE FIRST TIME I DID IT! AT NIGHT-TIME, WITH JUST THE ARTIFICIAL LIGHTS, I FELT LIKE AN URBAN GUERILLA!

2) BEFORE I LANDED, I MOVED MY BODY TO START PUSHING THE BIKE AROUND SIDEWAYS.

1) JUDGING YOUR SPEED IS IMPORTANT: YOU HAVE TO COME UP THE RAMP READY TO LAND ON YOUR BACK WHEEL IN BALANCE.

Dropping in at high speed.

4) FINISH THE 180° TURN AND COMMIT THE BIKE TO GOING BACK DOWN THE RAMP.

5) LET THE BACK WHEEL COME UP TO AVOID CATCHING IT ON THE EDGE.

3) LANDING ON THE BACK WHEEL, I'M ALREADY HALFWAY THROUGH THE TURN.

Being patched up after a fall at a competition.

13

AUGUST

2	9	16	23	30
3	10	17	24	31
4	11	18	25	
5	12	19	26	
6	13	20	27	
7	14	21	28	
1	8	15	22	29

RACER MIKE

Getting a good start is crucial.

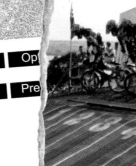

From: Mike Walters
To: Tyler Andrews
Subject: The true BMX
Date: Thursday, August 5

Hi Tyler! I don't know what my fool brother's been telling you about BMX racing, but he won't have got it right. So I thought I'd drop you an email to let you know what it's really like!

Basically, BMX racing is what all the other types of BMX grew out of. We ride bikes around a kind of dirt-bike obstacle course, with jumps and steep turns all round it. People originally used beach cruisers with 20" wheels, big balloon tires, a coaster brake and no gears. There's still a cruiser class in BMX comps here, but 'cruiser' now means a BMX with minimum 24" wheels.

There are three classes — novice, intermediate and expert. The classes are divided up by age, ranging from under-5 to over-18. The local racers all get to know each other, and it's a really good scene. If you don't believe me, give it a go!

See ya! Mike.

Found some cool BMX race words on an Internet site:

Holeshot The entrance to the first corner. Riders 'go for the holeshot', meaning they try to be first to the first corner.

Tabletop A jump with a flat top, like a table. Good riders take off using the up slope and land on the down slope.

Mike says BMX racing is a big crowd-pleaser in the US.

The racing's pretty fierce every weekend.

Download Manager

✓ BMX info.sit   Complete   < 1 minute

Basic BMX race bike rules:
- Must have 20" or less wheels (cruisers 24–26").
- No reflectors, axle pegs, chain guards or kick stands.
- Bikes must have a rear brake, either hand or coaster.
- Ends of handlebars must be covered.
- Top tube, stem and handlebar crossbar must be padded.
- Axles must not stick out more than 1/4"
- Number plates required.

15

AUGUST

2	9	16	23	30
3	10	17	24	31
4	11	18	25	
5	12	19	26	
6	13	20	27	
7	14	21	28	
1 (8)	15	22	29	

Check out my massive no-footer!

SKATEPARK

Just back from my first-ever visit to the big outdoor skatepark in the next town. We had an excellent time: compared to our usual spot this had a massive range of obstacles and ramps to practise on.

I was definitely glad to be wearing a helmet and pads, though. All those unfamiliar tricks meant I fell off my bike a lot, and it was really handy not to be scraping my knees and elbows all the time.

I wish we'd taken more to drink and eat with us. Spending a few hours riding in the sun, we seemed to get really thirsty. The drinks vending machine made a fortune out of us today!

THINGS TO LOOK OUT FOR AT THE SKATEPARK:

- Half-pipe — the most fearsome ramp in the park.
- Mini-ramp — popular, so it can take quite a long time to get a go. Really good for building your confidence.
- Handrail — lots of tricks you can do on this, but peg grinds are especially fun!
- Flatland area — why go to a skatepark to practise flatland skills? Because there are less cars than in your local car park, that's why!

It was the first time we'd been here. It's really popular with BMXers.

This boss 360 got a couple of whoops from the kids who were watching. As Dave says, 'Ride away with a big smile...'

SKATEPARK SATISFACTION

• Wait till the ramp or obstacle you want to use is clear before starting your approach.

• Always be aware of other users: don't try to intimidate people away from an obstacle. Everyone was a beginner once!

• Build up to bigger ramps: start small and let your confidence grow.

SEPTEMBER

	6	13	20	27
	7	14	21	28
1	8	15	22	29
2	9	16	23	30
3	10	17	24	
4	11	18	25	
5	(12)	19	26	

NO-HANDER DAY

Back at the skatepark for another big session – this time at one of the parks nearer to home. We got there without having to catch a train. Dave was riding really well, so I stopped hogging the ramp and took some photos of him doing a really good bus driver. Then I made him take photos of me doing an excellent no-hander (if I say so myself!).

TOP TIPS FOR A NO-HANDER:

This is a really spectacular jump, but judging your speed and the position of the bike in the air is crucial.

1 Coming out of the bowl, aim to get the bike heading up at a steeper angle than normal.

2 With the bike near vertical, release the bars, keeping your feet in contact with the pedals and the bike in front of you.

3 Bring your hands back to the bars and start to let the front of the bike move back towards horizontal.

4 Land on the back wheel, and ride away with a smile!

I only caught the second half of Dave's bus driver — I was too slow with the camera!

SEPTEMBER

6	13	20	27
7	14	21	28
1 | 8 | 15 | 22 | 29 |
2 | 9 | 16 | 23 | 30 |
3 | 10 | 17 | (24) | |
4 | 11 | 18 | 25 | |
5 | 12 | 19 | 26 | |

Warning! Flatlanding can result in injury...

FLATLANDING

Watching BMX videos round at Dave's house last weekend, we saw people riding 'flatland' for the first time. It's a way of riding your bike on flat ground (obviously!), using balance and bike control to make it do seemingly impossible things. The skill level of these guys was amazing — spinning their bikes around, leaping about on the back wheel, doing all kinds of complex switches around the front wheels of their bikes.

So, this evening after school we toddled off to a local park where there's a big section of smooth concrete. There were actually a couple of other guys there doing tricks too — we watched for a while, which is a really good way to work out how tricks are done, then had a go ourselves.

FLATLAND WORDS:

Bar flip When a rider spins his handlebars 180° or 360° during a front-wheel trick, landing back on the pegs.

Scuffing tricks Where the rider kicks ('scuffs') the wheel with his foot, to help him move and spin around.

Stoppie Rolling to a stop using balance and the front brake to keep the rear wheel in the air.

Wheelie The trick most people learn first: pedalling along with the front wheel in the air.

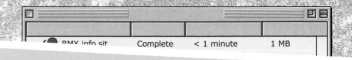

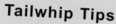

Tailwhip Tips

1 Roll up at a slow speed. When you're comfortable, lift your right foot over and stand on the wheel, between the fork and the tyre. Stop the bike on the front brake at the same time.

2 Kick the bike around with your left foot. As it starts to swing back, pull the bars towards you to maintain the swing's momentum.

3 As the bike returns to the starting point, grab the top tube with your 'free' left foot, stop it, and allow the back wheel to touch down. Pedal away.

It takes hours of practise to get this good.

A tailwhip in four easy stages.

OCTOBER

4	11	18	25
5	12	19	26
6	13	20	27
7	14	21	28
1 8	15	22	29
2 9	16	23	30
3 10	17	24	31

FIGHTING FIT

Week 3 of my fitness campaign: it's not exactly painless, but I'm starting to feel the benefits! There were three things I really wanted to improve on:

1) General fitness, so that I don't feel tired after an hour of riding.

2) Flexibility, so that it's easier to twist around and bend myself into shape for more complicated tricks.

3) Leg strength, so that I've got more acceleration on tap. Getting up to speed quicker would be really useful.

So: 1) running for leg strength and general fitness, 2) yoga for flexibility, and 3) eating better food (less sweeties and snacks; more apples and bananas – boo!) for all-round healthiness.

22

My leg strength and acceleration on the bike has definitely started to get a lot better since I started running.

Apparently it's important to eat a balance of these. Fats are also essential, but only in small quantities (like sweets!).

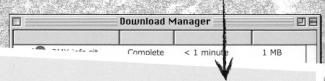

	Download Manager			
	Complete	< 1 minute	1 MB

Five major food groups

- Breads, cereals, rice and pasta
- Vegetables
- Fruits
- Milk, yogurt and cheese
- Meat, poultry, fish, dried beans and peas, eggs and nuts.

Being fitter has made it easier to concentrate on new tricks, instead of feeling tired.

I suppose if it wasn't painful it wouldn't be doing me any good!

I keep my hips level with the ground for this stretch, and don't arch my back.

This gives the muscles at the backs of your knees a stretch. Like the others, I hold it for a few breaths before stopping.

It's a good idea to relax your shoulders through stretching. Mustn't strain to stretch too far, though, or I'll get injured!

I hadn't realized I had muscles where this stretch pulls! It works well, though.

23

NOVEMBER

1	8	15	22	29
2	9	16	23	30
3	10	17	24	
4	11	18	25	
5	12	19	26	
6	13	20	27	
7	14	21	28	

COMPETITION

I have now officially caught up with Dave, because I just beat him in a comp! Actually I think I was really lucky. He tried a toothpick, which I know he can do, but it didn't quite come off. He fell over, and after that he just didn't ride well. Sometimes when you hit the deck you might as well just go home, because afterwards you just can't do anything but fall over again.

I went for easier tricks like peg grinds, with one tricky wall ride, and they all worked OK. In the end I came third. One of the riders from the shop I got my bike from beat me, and a guy I don't know. I give myself the same comment as on my school reports: acceptable, but 'could do better'!

This wall ride was my best moment.

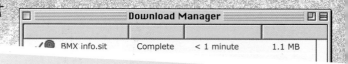

Download Manager				
BMX info.sit	Complete	< 1 minute	1.1 MB	

X-Games top ten riders, bike stunt, vert ramp, 2003
1. Jamie Bestwick 2. Dave Mirra
3. Kevin Robinson 4. Simon Tabron
5. Chad Kagy 6. John Parker
7. Dennis McCoy 8. Jimmy Walker
9. Eduardo Terreros 10. Koji Kraft

24

With the winner's cheque – I wish!

Dave Mirra

Nickname: Miracle Boy

Based: Greenville, NC, USA

Occupation: Pro rider

Riding since: 1981

Winner of 11 gold medals at the X-Games as well as taking various special-event titles. Dave is the world's best contest rider, and rarely finishes outside the top 6 in any vert or park contest.

Dave Mirra flying high.

HEROES

Rainy week in winter, so have been putting together a set of stats about my favourite riders in different BMX disciplines. It's amazing how long some of them have been the best riders around -- like Dave Mirra or Mat Hoffman. But there are new riders like Allan Cooke coming through all the time too.

Flatland: Martti Kuoppa

Born: 1978, Helsinki, Finland

Based: Helsinki, Finland

Occupation: Pro rider/co-owner of KGB Bikes

Riding since: 1991

Martti has been dominant in super-technical flatland competitions since about 2000. His innovative style and cutting-edge tricks make him a favourite with fellow riders, competition judges and video makers.

A massive dirt jump at Woodward, Pennsylvania.

Dirt riding: Stephen Murray

Born: 1980, Newcastle, England

Based: Corona, CA, USA

Occupation: Pro rider

Riding since: 1983

Rarely out of the top 6 in competition, his signature 360 tabletops and turndown flips are a result of an all-out attitude: 'I come to competitions to get first place, or last place', he says.

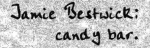
Jamie Bestwick:
candy bar.

Half-pipe: Jamie Bestwick

Born: 1971, Nottingham, England

Based: State College, PA, USA

Occupation: Pro rider

Riding since: 1981

He and Dave Mirra are the best half-pipe riders in the world today. Jamie threw the first-ever tailwhip flair seen in a competition, and uses more complex tricks than any other rider.

Steven McCann:
massive night-time
no-hander.

Spectacular
TJ Lavin
backflip.

BMX WORLDWIDE

BMX is a worldwide phenomenon! There are great riders all over the place, and fantastic locations for them to ride. This map shows highlights of just a few.

Rhode Island, USA

A whole range of street spots and ramps, hidden away on the USA's east coast.

Woodward, Pennsylvania

A big training camp in the USA — this is where you go if you want to get good, very quickly.

DIRT JUMPING

Lots of dirt jumping locations are hidden away in inaccessible woodlands. The woods of Pennsylvania, USA, and Surrey, England, are well-known locations, for example.

Austin, Texas, USA

A lively BMX scene means that the best street spots have been hunted out and worked, as well as videoed, many times.

Livingston, Scotland

Two legendary concrete skateparks that attract riders from all over the UK and beyond.

Meanwhile Gardens, England

East of London, this skatepark is a favourite with many southern-England BMXers.

Dusseldorf University, Germany

The unique architecture and design of the university's grounds and surroundings have made this a cult spot for BMXers from all over Europe.

Barcelona, Spain

A Mecca for skateboarders, BMXers, and other urban sports enthusiasts. Barcelona's mix of urban environments provides a massive range of obstacles, from long steps and handrails to concrete blocks.

Australia

Only the USA has more dirt-track BMX racers than Australia. Racers are found in all states and cities, including Adelaide (host of the 2004 championships) and Perth (which hosted the UCI BMX world championships in 2003). Street riding is also popular.

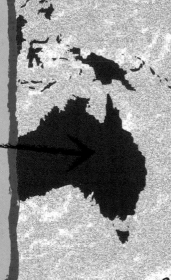

BMX WORDS

Bottom bracket
The device on the bike that allows the pedals and cranks to turn. The bottom bracket is fastened inside the bottom-most part of the frame.

Build-up
A bike that has been put together (built up) using the rider's choice of parts, instead of being supplied whole by the manufacturer.

Coaster brake
Also sometimes called a hub brake. Coaster brakes are hidden inside the hub of the back wheel. Pedalling backwards makes them come on. Once common on freestyle bikes, coaster brakes are now rarely used.

Cruiser
An American style of bike with big 'balloon' tyres, wide handlebars and a coaster brake.

Dirt
Riding on courses or jumps built of earth. Dirt courses are often hidden away in woodlands.

Dork
Someone who is unskilled at a particular activity.

Freestyle
A term that covers all aspects of BMX away from the racetrack.

Fufanu
Trick where rider hops on to their back wheel at the top of a ramp.

Grinds
BMX tricks where part of the bike – usually the trick pegs on the axles – is ground along an obstacle.

Half-pipe
A type of large ramp with very steep sides.

Momentum
Movement in a particular direction.

Park
A type of BMX riding and competition that takes place in a skatepark, using obstacles such as handrails, concrete blocks and single-sided jumps, but not the half-pipe or mini ramp.

Single-speed
A bike with only one gear.

Skatepark
An area designed and built for use by skateboarders, now usually used also by BMXers and inline skaters.

Special event
A one-off competition.

Street
Riding on the street, using obstacles such as kerbs and handrails to perform tricks.

Superman
A BMX jump where the rider sticks his or her legs out behind them, in an impression of the comic-book hero Superman flying through the air.

Trick

Can mean a stunt or skill; also used to describe something especially good or cool.

Vert

Describes a kind of riding that takes place on large half-pipes.

Wired

Understood really well, or worked out.

X-Games

An annual competition series made for TV. It has events around the world, showcasing BMX, skateboarding, snowboarding and other extreme sports.

INTERNET LINKS

www.bmxaustralia.com.au

Home site for Australian BMXers.

www.freedombmx.de

A German site, but in English. Good interviews with riders, as well as other BMX-related info.

www.expn.go.com

This site has really good profiles of riders, as well as some excellent trick tips for tricks ranging from a simple bunny hop to a toothpick or superman.

www.stpetebmx.com

A locally based site from St Petersburg in the USA, this nonetheless has good tips for beginner racers, and an excellent explanation of the skills and age group system.

www.pedalbmx.com

This site has message boards for all kinds of riding.

www.fatbmx.com

So current that this is where the magazines go to find out what's happening!

VIDEOS

Props video magazine is a bi-monthly video mag that features contests and information from around the world. Props also runs a 'Road Fools' series, featuring groups of top riders visiting a particular area.

MAGAZINES

DIGBMXMAG

Published monthly in the UK, this magazine has excellent international coverage of who's doing what, where, on the BMX scene.

Other magazines include **Ride** (UK), **Ride** (US), **Freedom** (Germany), **Cream** (France) and **Soul** (France).

DISCLAIMER

INDEX